A Pocket Full of Poesy

A tiny tome of epic proportions

by L. Jonté

ISBN: 0991558111

ISBN-13: 978-0991558117

"There's no money in poetry, but then there's no poetry in money, either."
- Robert Graves

FOREWORD

I feel I should state, before the question is asked: No, Like a Rose is not about any one particular person. No, really, so settle down. Not that I haven't known my share of the smug, the entitled, and the downright evil. I've logged an abundance of that kind of excruciating human contact, and will undoubtedly log a whole lot more. I just don't believe any one of those assholes deserves the spotlight of an entire dedicated work. Their antics are just fodder, not a feature.

Having said that, I will also say that I've always felt that an artist's works, like one's grown children, once set loose in the world, should be allowed to speak for themselves. Because, like one's grown children, no one is ever going to see them the way you do, (no matter how much you explain) so there's no point in trying. The best any artist, (or parent for that matter) can hope for is that eventually their work (or child) will meet with someone who loves them just as much.

-L. Jonté, February 1, 2014

CONTENTS

ARS BIBLIOS

Books are my family
And my furniture
They are my comfort
And my courage
They are my armor
When I must venture into the world
And my refuge
When I must escape it
They are temporal and telephonic
Transcendental and telepathic
Allowing anyone to hear the thoughts
Of those long dead or long away
With the turn of a page

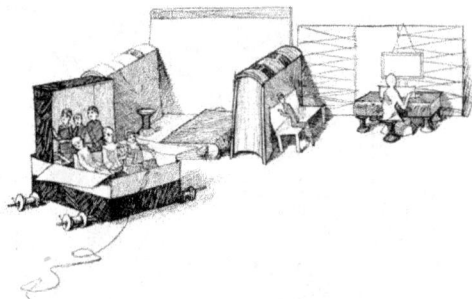

MY GOSPEL

All the saints in my heaven
Are drunkards and madmen,
Assailing the gates with
Pen and paper,
Brush and canvas,
Code and pixel;
This is my gospel.
To create, is the only religion I know.

LIKE A ROSE

Cerulean blue is the sky,
Reflecting across desert sand,
I hasten to bid you goodbye,
Your moment to go now at hand.

With everything packed in the car,
What little there is left to take.
Now hitched to a vagabond star,
A desolate life to remake.

I wince as you try not to cry,
My anger just barely at bay.
The both of us guarding the lie,
That neither knows just what to say.

But others are here with us too,
Unwitting, they feed the charade.
Unknown, the refusal by you,
To lie in the bed you have made.

Your modus was ever to cheat,
To smile as you twisted the knife.
Your saintliness, rankest deceit,
While secretly fostering strife.

I warned them of you, but in vain,
You had them beguiled from the start.
My envy, they told me, was plain,
And querulous too, was my heart.

Thus silently watching your dance,
Of friendly betrayal of trust,
I patiently waited my chance,
To grind all your intrigues to dust.

But fate it would seem, had a plan,
No effort I needed to make.
And now by your packed-up sedan,
You stand there, the consummate fake.

It's not the just ending I craved.
I'll take what I get, I suppose.
For all of your actions depraved,
You still came out smelling of rose.

So bid us your saddest farewell,
Dramatically playing your role.
I hope there's a chamber in Hell,
Reserved for your calcified soul.

THE TRUTH

I dream of rescues
And reprieves
I dream of that one, tactical notice that launches my abilities
into the stratosphere
Securing me real paying work and saving us
But the dream is a lie
And the truth is too important to lose
The truth is, if we are to survive, I'll have to do this myself
The truth is
Help isn't coming

AUTUMNAL INVOCATION

Spring be gone and summer too.
I bid your sunlit days adieu,
And gladly all your charms eschew.
I'm wholly sick of both of you

APPOINTMENT

The pumpkin's in the garden.
The cat is on the stair.
The ghost is in the graveyard.
And the monster's in her lair.

But when the leaves are turning and the summer's taken flight
These four all meet by moonlight on the last October night.

They meet for midnight revels
Beneath the autumn sky
To sing their odes and ballads
And drink the alehouse dry

It is the only night you see, that suits them all a'right
They may only meet by moonlight on the last October night.

The pumpkin's spied a shindig
The monster's taken point
Cat and ghost are eager
To fall about the joint

They ravage bar and buffet, then they give the host a fright
Then stagger 'neath the moonlight on the last October night.

Caution tossed upon the winds
They terrorize and tease
Roaming town and country
And doing as they please

In scandalous diversion, they take the most delight
The four who meet by moonlight on the last October night.

You may have your tricks-or-treats
In costumes cheap or dear.
Naught can match the party
That they have once a year.

They are a merry, raucous band until the morning light
Those four who meet by moonlight on the last October night.

Perchance some year you'll see them
On distant field or lawn
Hie yourself away then
Unless it's near the dawn.

Their powers only fade beneath November's dawning bright.
They are only meant for moonlight on the last October night.

IN THE GARDEN

In the garden of the valley of the houses of the dead
Flow the whispers of confessions of a thousand things unsaid.
Yond the shutters come a'peeping twice a thousand sightless eyes
At once comical and mirthless, watching as I pass, unwise.
Some are standing some are sitting each one mocking living pose
Some with books and some at table, passing each, my terror grows.
Desiccated are the neighbors, dusty husks and rictus grins,
All grotesquery and silence, aping mortal chores and sins.
Now my heart is quicker beating I can scarcely draw a breath
As I hasten for an exit from this living world of death.
Though my progress is unfettered and the watchers do not stir
Still I cannot shake the feeling that my stay here will endure.
Both in waking and in dreaming must my footfalls ever tread
In the garden of the valley of the houses of the dead.

INVOCATION

Winter comes, the earth to wed.
To ice she yields her maidenhead.
But ere the skies are turned to lead,
and all the world is quieted,
bestir the sleeping still abed,
those gone before yet gone ahead.
With joyful noise no shade we dread.
Let our revels wake the dead!

This poem originally appeared in the webcomic I was creating
at the time: **Arcana Jayne**

AN EARLY WINTER'S TALE

The stars were ice, the wind did blow
It whispered songs of early snow
Among the trees where spirits glow
And mortal men are a'feared to go
Yet she passed there alone

All on this crystal cold midnight
Beneath the Autumn Eve's moonlight
Upon her steed of whitest-white
Did Lady Paladin alight
The one who had no name

From sharp, dark eyes to visage grim
To red-brown hair and body trim
Not one detail was lost on him
The one who watched from far tree limb
He smiled with rakish glee

As through the oaken grove she rode
Amid the thorn and dyer's woad
Her thoughts they bore a heavy load
Of bloody deeds and honor owed
She noted not the path

Her horse's hooves had found a dale
Thick with mist and moonlight pale
Unnoticed, somewhere, on that trail
They'd lost the sounds of nightingale
And other earthly calls

She paid no heed, nor wary care
No thought for who or what lived there
And thus was she caught unaware
And captured in a Faery snare
The Lady was undone

She struggled vainly there and then
'Gainst horrid little goblin men
Who reeked of gasses from the fen,
As they'd not bathed since who-knew-when
In numbers, they were strong.

Pulled beneath the earthy dome
Of soil and bracken, roots and loam
Far beneath her mortal home
A pris'ner lost in catacomb
She stilled herself to think

She heard no horse nor bridle ring
Her horse, it seemed, had taken wing
No hope of aid on which to cling
The goblin brutes began to sing
Their voices sharp and shrill

"Bound with ropes of eldrich-make
This mortal to our King we take
May he reward us all with cake
Baked with bones dredged from the lake!"
"Ah-loo! Ah-loo! Ah-loo!"

The goblin goons of Faeryland
All pulled and tugged by hair and hand
The Lady 'cross the muddy sand
Of subterranean lake-shore strand
Her patient anger grew

Her transport fast came to a close
With thumps and bumps and goblin blows
With armor bent and bloodied nose
Refused to kneel, instead she rose
And faced the Faery King

Handsome, tall and pale as milk
This elfin man of noble ilk
And with a voice as smooth as silk
He smiled and said, "My name is Ryll'kh."
Then lightly kissed her brow

"You'll not hold me for long," she said
"Soon either you or I'll be dead."
Then wiped his kiss off of her head
He smiled and laughed, "Your face is red!
But I've no wish to fight."

"You think for me a ransom then?
For riches not of Faery ken?"
The King's light smile said 'Wrong again.'
He wanted naught from mortal men
She knew now what he meant

He made a gesture, spoke a sound
Her armor now could not be found
But garbed in velvet all around
Her hair, now clean, was fancy bound
He kissed her hand and spoke

"Come walk with me about the lea
A dark moon shines on Undersea
All this and more I'll gift to thee
But you must stay below with me
In body, mind and soul

The Faery King then pulled her near
Her soft assent he meant to hear
He heard instead a whispered sneer
"I'll never marry you 'my dear'
My life is mine to rule."

"Thy Lord I now, and ever, am
My dearest, sweetest mortal lamb
This bravado girl, is but a sham
Your preference matters not a damn
I will have your submission."

"Deist, O' Lord of roots and mold
For I, all honor must uphold
My heart cannot be bought nor sold
With meager threats, or minor gold
Your petty scheme will fail."

"And more," the Lady ventured still
"Your efforts here to force my will
have set your life's value at nil
A shallow grave, with you, I'll fill
Alert your next of kin."

"Tempt not my ire, O' willful cow!
Let rats become thy bedmates now
And all too soon will you learn how
To serve your King and meekly bow
"Lock her in the dungeon!"

A gesture from the King revealed
The armor that had been concealed
Now clad again for battlefield
Though still, she had no sword to wield
But helpless, she was not

The trollish guards then moved in fast
But faster still, her spell was cast
The trolls engulfed in hellish blast
All knew that they had breathed their last
The Faery court stood silent

"Magnificent!" Did Ryll'kh declare
"Thy rage has made thee yet more fair
I'll have you in my bed I swear
And get from you a mighty heir
Now come my love, relent!"

"Relent? Have you gone mad?" She said
"Your trollkin guards are smoking dead
Yet still you think to gain my bed
Now get this through your elvish head
I am no one's chattel!"

Before another word was spoke
Across the Faery hall she broke
She left behind a cloud of smoke
And scores of baffled elverfolk
She found her way and ran

The King let out an outraged cry
And called the goblins standing by
"Stop her ere she tries to fly
Or I shall know the reason why!"
His tone brooked no denial

Gnashing teeth and lashing tail
The goblin henchmen keen and wail
"Broken bones for all who fail
To catch her ere she gains the dale!"
The goblin horde gave chase

Knowing that she could not win
Fighting King and Faery kin,
She could not smite his cocky grin
If, his realm, she stayed within
She raced for mortal soil

Hounded by the goblin band
Past the muddy lake-shore strand
Across the shining shadow-land
She'd reach her world then take a stand
She knew what she must do

But if she were to reach the dell
The goblin band she first must quell
She turned her head and threw a spell
That knocked them all halfway to Hell
Weary, she kept running

Heeding the unholy sound
Of his lecher's blood go pound
Ryll'kh had gathered horse and hound
To chase her through the Faery mound
He summoned too, the Host

Across the land of in-between
The host flowed slick and serpentine
A'glowing 'neath the dark moon's sheen
Like mist made flesh; blue, white and green
A sight to chill the blood

Though she could feel the hunt draw near
Their calls and howls now filled her ear
The Lady had no thoughts of fear
But only of her homeland dear
At last she'd found her way

Finally, out of Faery ken
But standing in that selfsame glen
Whence she'd been dragged into their den
She found her horse, her sword and then
Prepared for those behind

Once ready, then, she watched the soil
Grim, as it began to roil
And churn like water on the boil
Exploding forth the Faery coil
Ryll'kh among the first

For a blink the earth stood still
A heartbeat's time to set her will
One second of eternal chill
An instant caught and held until
The time to strike had come

Through a fire-and-brimstone blast
She burst upon the scene at last
And with a move uncanny-fast
She faced the King., the die was cast
"Fight me Ryll'kh, or die."

"Fight thee?" Said the King, alarmed
"But you have not been truly harmed
Besides," he said. "I am unarmed
Thy passions too, have me quite charmed
Come kiss me and be done!"

"You crave a kiss?" She whispered low
"Then such a kiss I shall bestow."
Her armored fist then pulled back, so
And 'kissed' him with a crushing blow
He saw it, but too late

Her 'soldier's kiss' had left him numb
Better had he been struck dumb
For presently his tirade come
In language purple as a plum
Obscenities, fast flowing

Screaming from his bloody face
He called for backup from his race
Stock still, they would not move a pace
"This combat, we will not disgrace
The challenge: Thine alone."

"Alone!?" he spat, past blood and gore
"I am ye King and this is war!
Obey me as was done of yore
And kill this armored, mortal whore!"
A murmur stirred crowd

A single Lord stepped from the rest
And laid a hand upon his breast
"T'was you that stole her from her quest
Thus you alone must pass this test."
"Come! Give the King his sword."

Then to Her the Elf Lord turned
His visage cool and unconcerned
But past his eyes a fire burned
And 'neath his calm a tempest churned
He nodded and withdrew

"T'would seem your people," Lady said
"Are most exceedingly well bred
Would that you'd followed where they led
You brought this all upon your head
But honor will be served."

They clad their King in Faery mail
Contrived to look like dragon-scale
His sword was sheer and cobweb-pale
And carved with runes in great detail
It shone with arcane light

Though muck and mire from toes to hair
The Lady still was comely-fair
Despite the long day's wear and tear
She held herself with regal air
And drew her own bright sword

Without a warning Ryll'kh's hand lashed
But Lady's sword, as quickly, flashed
And blade on blade, like thunder, crashed
Ryll'kh's hope of easy vict'ry dashed
She met him blow for blow

"Foolish girl," he gave a sneer
"Thou shouldst not have stayed so near
My realm continues, even here
You'll pay for that mistake my dear."
The Lady only smiled

The King incanted spells of old
For nature's fury uncontrolled
And waited for it to unfold
But no rain fell, no thunder rolled
The night was still and calm

"I arrived here first," She said
"And harvested a yarrow bed
And hawthorn berries, rich and red
They're strewn across the ground we tread
To ward off Faery spells."

The scoundrel King was quite a sight
His face was now a bloodless white
He screamed defiance to the night
But in the end his choice was flight
He dropped his sword and ran

Then Ryll'kh, retreating through the crowd
Half blind, into the Elf Lord plowed
The smiling Lord crooned, "Not allowed!"
Then to the grim swordswoman, bowed
And shoved Ryll'kh back to her

A flourish brought her sword to bear
It grazed his throat but halted there
He squirmed beneath her icy glare
As sweat began to mat his hair
"Surrender Ryll'kh. I've won."

"This battle may be thine," he said
"But one day thou wilt warm my bed
Then by my hand you will be dead!"
The Lady merely shook her head
He'd left her with no choice

A saddened sigh escaped her lips
She tensed from toes to fingertips
"King, it's time you came to grips
You'll start no more kidnap-courtships
Prepare, your fate is done."

Realization struck his soul
He tried a frantic tuck-and-roll
But Lady's sword had found its goal
As morning's bells began to toll
He fell without a groan

His life's-blood spilt upon the grass
The Host intoned his funeral mass
They dubbed him ever, 'Ryll'kh the Crass.'
"More like Ryll'kh the Silly Ass."
The Elf Lord muttered low

Fragile sunlight; pale and wan
Proclaimed that day was but anon
With that wispy kiss of dawn
The Faery Horde and Host were gone
The Elf Lord only, stayed

A trace of sadness crossed his face
He said, "No one will give thee chase
But better now to leave this place
Thou art a credit to thy race
I wish thee naught but well."

"One final word, O'Lady Wise."
A look of anguish filled his eyes
"As I am King, with Ryll'kh's demise.
Allow me to… apologize
Thy capture was my fault."

"Thy travels near were known to me
I spied, concealed within a tree
Once Ryll'kh learned I admired thee
He acted with vindictive glee
And took you for himself."

She arched a single dark eyebrow
Observed the new King's humble bow
And said, "I care not why nor how
Nor who has caused this royal row
Best leave it in the past."

"But keep this as a lesson taught
Should I hear of other women caught
In Faery snares, your life is naught
I'll cut you down without a thought
And your kingdom with you

She turned and spurred her horse to go
The morning sun gave way to snow
Among the trees where spirits glow
And mortal men are a'feared to go
And she left there alone

The Elf King gestured hand and wrist
And blew to her a breeze he'd kissed
He turned then with an agile twist
And vanished, smiling, in the mist
Winter had come early

A final word of thanks to one Steve Barker, patient friend and valiant defeater of terrifying walls of instructional text. I owe you more than you will ever admit you deserve.

ABOUT THE AUTHOR

Writer & Editor of many things; prose, poetry, comics, columns, and reviews. Have opinions. Will travel.

www.ingramcontent.com/pod-product-compliance
Lightning Source LLC
Chambersburg PA
CBHW060548030426
42337CB00021B/4494